Desire & Power
Poetry and Subtext

Poetry chapbooks by Kim Bayer

- Fractions of Destiny Collection of Poetry
- Definitions of Beauty:
Capturing the Essence of Beauty in Twenty Poems

*Intuitive and counter-intuitive,
sometimes desire seeks power,
other times power seeks desire.*[1]

Copyright © 2013 by Kim Bayer
ISBN 978-1-304-20892-7
Vancouver, BC
www.fractionsofdestiny.com

Cover photo © Andrew Jo
jyongin@gmail.com

---

[1] This collection of poetry draws from the graduate studies thesis project *Examining Desire: Meanings, Measurements and Musings* (Bayer, 2012).

Black & White Photos
© Lisa Bayer
www.lisabayer.com

With sincere appreciation to Lisa
and the men and women in these photos
for their fearlessness and willingness
to share their image,
often in the most intimate moments.

Kim Bayer, July 2013

Introduction |6|
Measuring Desire |8|
Desire as Reflex |11|
Desire and Addiction |16|
Desire and Power |21|
Desire and Trauma |26|
Desire and the Impulse to Protect |30|
Desire and the Imprints of History |32|
Desire Across Time |38|
Philosophical Underpinnings of Desire i-x |45|
   i. Delirium & Drift |46|
   ii. Desiring Machines |50|
   iii. Circular Movement |55|
   iv. Rational & Representative Desires |58|
   v. Shapes & Connections: Self-Returned From Other |65|
   vi. To Know is to Desire |68|
   vii. Reflectivity & Desire |72|
   viii. Altering Desire |75|
   ix. Dreams & Desires |79|
   x. Freudian Shortcomings |87|
Desire and Artistic Expression |92|
Desire and the Changing Seasons |97|
Closing Thoughts |102|

Introduction

At this point in time, within our mass media-driven world, which has been co-opted by the immediacy of cyberspace, the experience of desire often conjures up images of clichéd passion and sexed-up innuendo. Yet in actuality, desire crosses a vast array of psychical landscapes; sometimes brief and fleeting or, conversely, the result of profound and life-altering events. Other times it is tenacious and unshakable, rooted deep within the heart and psyche. Either way, beyond the first-glance, predictable facets of desire its core impulse is to resolve tension, diminish distance, and satiate needs.

The compulsion to sabotage beauty or, alternatively, the search for beauty and resolve, even when constrained by the darkest depths of emotional pain, as well as the re-assembly of missed or severed connections also reflect desire's impulse. In this way, desire is a catalyst for movement, journey, and history.

In this collection of poetry I explore the fluid layers of desire to reveal its changeable nature, which shapes over time and experience. Through these revelations, I weave links between desire and reflex (biology), desire and addiction, trauma, time/seasons and history, and desire and power. As well, I explore desire and the impulse to protect, desire and art, and desire's philosophical underpinnings.

My hope is that within these pages you find traces of your own desire history, which awakens new understanding of your own subtext.

Measuring Desire

The measurement of desire through its capacity to resonate, even dominate our existence, is contingent on *who* is measuring its dimensions, including psychologists, philosophers, artists, writers, or even love-struck individuals.

In general, there are two modes of desires: Acquired desires, which vary across individuals, and natural desires, which are both pervasive and inherent to the human experience.[2]

Lover's desire is familiar to most of us; it speaks to the acquisitive nature of desire, when we are driven by our impulses and compelled to satisfy them. It also reflects a lack of presence, an empty space, with pleasure as its units of measure.

---

[2] Adler, M. (1991). *Desires: Right & Wrong.* New York: Macmillan.

Two Years Later

Two years later
she was still there, waiting
while he, standing there, arms crossed
hiding his breath
relief-flavored gin and wine
calming emotions
fuelled by chaos and
need for control.

They indulged in the moment
reckless and forgetting
he took pleasure knowing
she used his body
the same way he used
gin and ale to paralyze.

Morning stabbed her
with emptiness, silently
she condemned him
his sickening habit and
the cheap part she played
in the melodrama.

Two years later
she was still there, waiting...

Desire as Reflex

The human desire for sexual pleasure is attributed to a reflex response intrinsic to our genetic system, which serves to preserve our species rather than our individual impulses.

The pleasure of sexual touch urges the human body to reproduce, ensuring its genes survive into future generations.[3] But without some level of control over our desires other goals become blocked.

Desire and self-sabotage:
When we abandon our own needs, interests
or even survival instincts,
believing this will bring us closer to the object
of our desires and, in this closeness,
all missing emotional pieces
will be found.

---

[3] Csikszentmihalyi, M. (1990). Chapter 1: Happiness revisited. In *Flow: The psychology of optimal experience* (pp.1-22). New York: Harper Perennial.

Role Play - 1

Warm breath on cold window
and eager bodies that curve over
the back of a tattered couch
as bright and impatient eyes wait
for the moment when daddy's car
will pull into the driveway; at last
gravel crunches beneath wheels
home sweet home
three hundred miles is forever
when you're four and six years old.

It is nearly dark when the car door slams
and familiar footsteps bring elated smiles
to his restless and waiting children.
She is hopeful it will be different this time
but the truth wells up within her—
it will always be the same.

Relieved and overjoyed
they run to him, while he
puts on a happy face
heavy with Jack Daniels
that got to him first.

She surrenders
pours herself a strong one
that leads to another
altering reality with a frame-by-frame
hazy distortion that blends
in with the talk, the play, the neediness
as they plead their case to stay up—
one more show, one more game,
one more turn.

He stands by the door
with eyes that seek
forgiveness and second chance
or third, or thirty-something
(she can't remember any more).
She is torn. The sensation in her belly
is a free-falling flutter into a knot of chaos
the gutter of hope, buried by the pain
of waiting too long for too little
"Stay", she says, "It's late."

Beside her
he drifts into the comfort of sleep
while she tosses and turns
restless and unresolved
until morning wakes him
to slip into old habits
caressing the curve of her hip.
Her body responds.
She is both repulsed and awakened
by his deep breath, his animal-like sighs
numb and silent to the rote surrender.

She hears the children at the table
pouring Cheerios in bowls
clanging spoons from the drawer
watching Saturday cartoons.

She slinks into the shower
closes her eyes as
water cascades down
pulling tears with it.
But this time is different:
She cannot cleanse
the violent sickness
and hollow emptiness
of this worn and tired role play.

.

Desire and Addiction

Desire acted upon without boundaries can slip into addictive-like impulses. The individual with no bounds on desires for alcohol, food, or sex becomes hostage to these excesses and, consequently, susceptible to the exploitation of others.[4] Ironically, instead of satiating the need to resolve distance, across time, desire addiction creates greater emotional distance.

*"A single rogue desire
can trample the plans we had for our lives
and thereby alter our destinies."*[5]

---

[4] Csikszentmihalyi, M. (1990).

[5] Irvine, W. (2006). *On desire: Why we want what we want.* New York: Oxford University Press. p.11.

Role Play – II

This is no disguise.
It is more like a brave front
a suit of armor changed into
as dark shadows are cast
when the doubting erupts
and the mind disrupts
pulled between truth and
the recurring lie, perseverating,
"I alone could never be enough."

It is the actor within, engaged, on stage,
a creative form of assimilation
a blending of the outside and inside
of pleasing Other and mother
and lastly the often-silent self
steadfast and slowly seeping through.

Amoeba Joe

Forever changeable
that is what you are;
it traces back to childhood
living in a home with a father
a raging alcoholic, controlling
a mother who stayed in the trap
because all she'd ever known was
poverty, struggle, and desertion.

To survive the dysfunction
you learned to adapt
until the day you came home
to find your father in bed
with your mother's best friend.
Raging with betrayal, you confronted him
in turn, he unleashed a full assault
of knife-wielding fury on you.
Bloodied and defeated, fifteen years old,
you left home and never looked back.

Now you repeat this death
of a dream of love, over and over
you seek the dependency of a woman
just like your mother (compliant)
and when you find her

as soon as she is weakened by
your convincing spell of love
she is dropped; she is no longer desired.
You become violent, like your father,
then sickened by the resemblance
you waver back and forth
between roles of dominance
neediness, and indifference
all the while only seeking
to be desired, so you repeat again
because *the next time will be different*
(said the addict)
the next time will be the endgame
where all the anger subsides
where the impulse to chase desire
catch and release
dissolves
into something that resembles
peace, forgiveness, and acceptance.

Again and again, the inner wound that needs healing rises to the surface, making itself known.

Desire and Power

The roots of desire can always be traced to individual needs for power. In the human ego, which is influenced by the external world, power is a mechanism for control. The only person indifferent to power is the person who is indifferent to people in general.[6]

In intimate relationships, the learned behavior of codependency emerges when the *controller* and the *controlled* mesh their polarizing forces. The *controller*, once in charge, will never relinquish power. The *controlled*, previously broken and now submissive, assumes position. Like some twisted form of yin and yang, paradoxically, even across a crowded room, each will always find each other.

The struggle to gain control is perpetual.
Like a prized possession, the be-all and end-all,
first we struggle to gain control,
then we fight to maintain control
and, once lost, we fight to regain upper hand.

---

[6] Russell, B. (1930). *The conquest of happiness.* New York: W.W. Norton & Company.

Hiding and Seeking

Slowly, she walks
Raymur and Cordova Streets
near the grass-covered railway tracks
now abandoned and grey-spirited
through the garbage-strewn lanes
by the run-down industrial buildings.
She stops. Then paces back
to the edge of the block in short strides
her eyes both hiding and seeking.

It is payday Friday, five o'clock
she knows some of the regulars
will come around looking for her
and just as she thinks this
John pulls around the corner
in his rusted brown pick-up truck
his eyes both hiding and seeking.

He drives closer to her
rolls down the window to say hello
with cold piercing eyes
and a pressing need to dump pieces
of his dreary life onto someone
in no position to resist.

Cool and collected, he is in control
while she positions herself near
the window on the passenger side.
He drives behind the metalwork shop
then cuts the engine as he reaches into
the glove box for a bag of marijuana.
He rolls a joint and makes small talk
complaining about his boss and his ex-wife;
she has heard this story, or ones just like it
(the details interchangeable)
a hundred times before.
She, now an actress in a role,
nods her head, too tired to feign interest.

The ritual for the violation begins:
In her mind, part of her body
leaves the vehicle, transformed
to a safer place, while the rest
of her remains behind, contained
like a hunted animal in survival mode.

Depleted of talk, he moves to
the final purge of powerlessness—
the opening of a condom, her cue
to begin jerking and sucking his penis
as he moves his calloused hand
over the back of her head
pushing down hard, rhythmically,
like a desperate controlling machine.

Later, he drops her off
by the corner store
to buy pop and cigarettes
and drives off into
the polluted sunset
one hazy-bright orb
in his mundane world.

As she leaves the store
she runs into some kids she knows
from the housing complex down the way
"Hi, Ashley", one of the girls says to her,
"I like your skirt, you look pretty today."
She says thanks and is on her way
back to the lanes, back to where
no other man will notice anything
beautiful about her.
For them, this is the point.

Desire and Trauma

Traumatic events trigger varying degrees of psychological harm and suffering. Even though chronic abuse can cause lasting harm, one single devastating experience can also become the initial wound of a painful emotional scar.

Therapeutic interventions strive to help victims reconstruct fragments of memory and history, and shed light on the meaning of present symptoms with past experiences. This is not an easy task, as it involves facing human vulnerability and the capacity for evil in human nature.[7]

Not all victims have access to healing supports. As a result, beginning with the first wound, a web of trauma and desire begins to weave intricate layers of pain, coping mechanisms, and acts of survival.

However, trauma is not always obvious to loved ones, or even the victim, because sometimes a disconnect exists between actions and outcomes. For example, the child who grows up in a family where there is tension and conflict between parents takes in this dysfunction. Resilience, then, merely becomes an outward appearance. On a deeper level,

---

[7] Herman, J. (1997). *Trauma and recovery: The aftermath of violence – from domestic abuse to political terror.* New York: Basic Books.

the victim of this conflict feels insecure, anticipates a lack of support from others, or other self-defeating behaviors. Often, in an effort to re-script this experience, the victim repeats the learned parental relationship pattern in his/her own intimate relationships. Sadly, without new insight and healing, the outcome is similar: Unsatisfied desires and strained relationships.

A Reason to Run

Even as a child you were a thinker
sensitive, intuitive, creative
a teacher's dream student
yet never really noticed
quiet and steadfast
your peaceful nature
taken for granted
blended into the background.

Your parents were good people
working long hours, checking off
the boxes of life: a mortgage and bills
a new station wagon every few years;
neglecting the desires of their own heart
without notice, they neglected yours.

Now you're on stage every night
singing songs about love and pain
when all you really want
is to be desired
when everyone loves you
everything will be alright
all the suffering will have meaning
you will be victorious.

All these things give you reason to run—
you run to the woman with the closed heart
you run from the woman with open arms;
with all your desires, still, you run.

Desire and the Impulse to Protect

Often desire is an experience so profound in nature that it coincides with an impulse to protect the innermost details of intimacy. Exposing the details of intimacy is comparable to betrayal.

As each experience of desire is distinct, desire is preserved best when claimed as new, each time, in each new body as there is no relevance across the divide that separates one generation from another.[8]

Although an impulse to protect desire exists, there is no reason to shelter desire with silence. True desire is not always easily contained, simply because unspoken desire cannot always conceal its appetitive, large-looming power and presence. We read desire in others; its vibrant resonance is unmistakable. When attraction-desire floats into the room every intuitive person knows.

"Intimacy is the place where desire thrives."[8]

---

[8] Burnard, B. (1999). Silence and exception. In *Desire in seven voices* (Lorna Crozier, Ed.). pp. 87-103. Vancouver, BC: Douglas & McIntyre.

The Invisible Wall

A forty-something mother
second generation of matriarchs
to live in this three-story bungalow
walks up the wooden stairs
pausing mid-step
startled by sobbing sounds
coming from her daughter's room.

A mother's instinctive need to comfort
calls her toward the closed-door room
in the hall, she stops, resting her head
on the flower-patterned wallpaper
waiting for the resolution of silence
saddened, when it does not come.
She moves closer to the pain...
softly cracking the door ajar
her sixteen-year old daughter, Lily
on the bed, holding a photo of a boy
two years older. wiser. freedom-seeker.

Intuitively sensing her mother's presence
Lily turns away, hiding denied desire
and a tear-stained face. alone. unwilling
to let her mother in
to a place she's already known.

Desire and the Imprints of History

Desire interweaves with cultural and generational history, and traces of this find expression in our current experiences. The recognition of this history is what brings desire to consciousness.[9] Sometimes we experience this as déjà vu; a kind of delightful, momentary jolt of familiarity, recognizing its presence, even though the full meaning of its significance is not yet known.

Paradoxically, desire reveals our relationships
to distance and difference (lack)
and familiarity
(knowledge, history and blood memories).

---

[9] Brand, D. (1999). Arriving at desire. In *Desire in seven voices* (Lorna Crozier, Ed.). pp. 125-142. Vancouver, BC: Douglas & McIntyre.

Mirror and Landscape

When I was ten years old
I discovered a post-war
sepia-toned photo of my Métis uncle
his eyes sad and knowing.
There was more—
a weathered history within his eyes
like a mirror and a landscape
reflecting back to me
something familiar within
and something significant to come.

Now my innocence was lost.
Once known, there is no return
to the time of oblivious bliss.
I carry traces of this truth forward…

Sixteen years old, with a driver's license
promising sweet freedom and escape
far beyond the confines of suburbia
I remember one night
driving with two guy friends, one my age
and an older drinking-age friend
cruising Vancouver's Downtown Eastside
and its streets of human suffering
petty crime and concrete decay.

As we drove by the run-down hotel strip
the older friend mocked the Native women
and the half-breeds like me blending in
with the crowd, working as prostitutes.

Seemingly empowered by their plight
he rattled off the rates they charged
for various sexual activities
as my heart skipped a beat.
The low place and value of Métis women
confirmed, in my sixteen-year-old mind,
that I could no longer identify as Métis
could no longer be associated with
such a down-trodden destiny.
I had no value. My *Indianness*
made it certain, I would not be desired
and I thought of my uncle's sad eyes...

From that moment on
and for many years to come
I despised
the slightly slanted shape of my eyes
and the white-brown patchiness of my skin
that made me neither fully white nor fully
Indian.
I was stained
by *white people's* misperceptions

of what it meant to be Métis
I had no power to change
the history of this stain.

Three years ago
I met a Native man
his eyes familiar
deep and sad;
they called me closer
they called me to my inner voice
searching for healing.

He awoke early one morning
to quietly gather his things
then reached over to kiss me.
I said nothing, knowing
it was a final goodbye.

Six months later, he called.
I did not respond.
I could not re-open old wounds again.
I could not play the power-struggle
relationship-physics game with my heart—
when he senses I want intimacy, he pulls away.
Desire must be his idea.
The history of his own desire
tells him this is so.

Lighter Now

I am lighter now
that time has passed
from the moment where
pain rocked every cell
in my broken and defeated body.

Each frame of the moment
is seared within my mind's eye:
Morning had barely broken
its soft light seeping in
to the side of the shade.

On the edge of the bed
you reached for your keys
as I turned to caress a line
down your back (for the last time).
You turned to catch my eyes
with a closed-mouthed smile
the intuition on my lips said
it's over. Over.

Although the door closed softly
sound resonated with finality;
at first, I am sickened and broken...
later, the sun rises across the sky
I realize I am lighter now.
Lighter now.

Desire Across Time

Desire has a powerful capacity to be re-imagined or re-ignited at any point in time; it has a lasting history that seeps into the present, its commanding presence written into the chapters of life as indelible and distinct traces of memory on the heart and in the body.[10]

Desire, an unpredictable agitator, returns at random, tapping on the door of memory, wanting back in, stirring sleeping emotions, demanding attention like a restless child refusing to be ignored.[10]

---

[10] Crozier, L. (1999). Changing into fire. In *Desire in seven voices* (Lorna Crozier, Ed.). pp. 63-85. Vancouver, BC: Douglas & McIntyre.

Distraction and Reality

He moved back to Seattle
after she left.
Day in and day out
the rain and concrete
helped to distract him
from thoughts of her.

He spent his days
writing for a magazine
his nights taking courses
his weekends hanging out
with old friends.

Two summers later
he came back to Vancouver.
While hanging out at Kits Beach
he saw her walking with a friend
just as she recognized him
cool and moved on, he turned away.

"Hey, she said,
"Nice to see you.
Are you working in Vancouver?"

He can't recall his response
only that her presence
stirred every cell in his body.
Maybe he was not so
moved on.
Maybe it was just
a conditioned response
to pleasures once known.

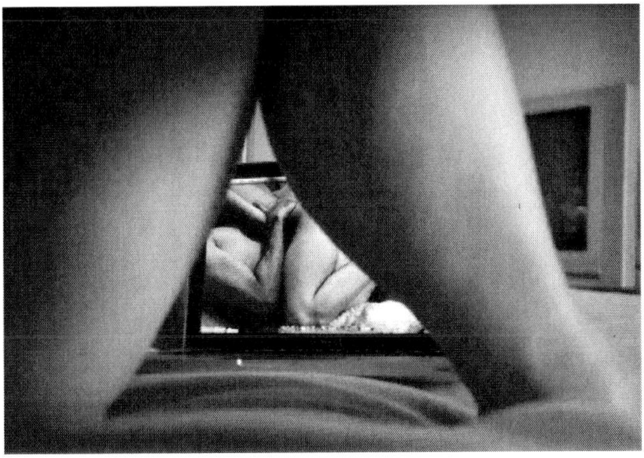

Thirst

Desire does not lend itself to being
fixed up or cleaned up, instead
it interweaves with past and present.
Yet the human capacity to tolerate
the sting of broken-heartedness
and chronic, sustained desire drama
is not without limits.

>The gaping hole of defeat
>of missed connections
>cannot be filled.
>But admitting
>we have longed for
>the *wrong* desire or
>cannot satiate our desires
>leaves us feeling
>deprived and depleted.
>
>We remain determined
>to fix *this*; we try again
>hoping it will be different
>giving second and third chances
>to someone who can't receive
>our desire.

We move to plan B.
We find someone
a facsimile, just like the other
and try again.

In futility
we blame others
afraid of the mirror
unwilling to go to the place
that reveals the truth
of why we frantically
chase the impossible
the elusive desire.
Could it simply be
we want to re-write
the story of
the one that got away?
Silly human ego.

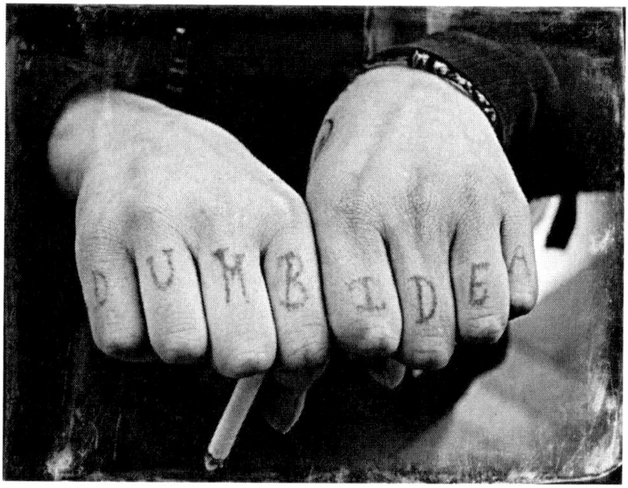

Philosophical Underpinnings
of Desire
i. ~ x.

i. Delirium & Drift

One theory of desire is that a feeling of *lack* forms from rational, social influences, while *desire* forms from irrational sources, and is always positive.[11] Although society convinces us to find love and live happily-ever-after, a seemingly rational pursuit, its prescriptive interference with our desire selection often leads to the oppression of individual desires.

However, as we await the arrival of our soul mate we sometimes feel the emptiness of missed desires. In the meantime, our heart may lead us to all kinds of unanticipated places, with its tendency to drift to irrational but desire-kindled places. As a result, "underneath all reason lies delirium and drift."[12]

With unrest and confusion hovering just beneath the surface, and without some form of gate-keeping, the sick and twisted undercurrent of society seeps into our desires. Society, as a mega-machine of successive, historical social forms, ensures this works both ways: Society sickens people and sick people are vulnerable to its diseased ways.

---

[11] Desire theory of Gilles Deleuze, a twentieth century French philosopher.

[12] Smith, D. (2007). Deleuze and the question of desire: Toward an immanent theory of ethics. *Parrhesia: A Journal of Critical Philosophy*, 2.

Sick and Twisted

Alan Turing
ground-breaking
computer scientist
Princeton mathematician
and government code-breaker
back in 1952
the British post-war era
when homosexuality was illegal;
after charges of gross indecency
he chose chemical castration
over the confines of prison.[13]

Society called him sick and twisted.
Society, the great oppressor,
is sick and twisted
cold and unforgiving
restrained by lies and ties
to old church traditions.

---

[13] Halberstam, J. (1991). Chapter 26: Automating Gender (pp.468-483). In P. Hopkins (Ed.). *Sex/Machine: Readings in culture, gender, and technology.* Bloomington, IN: Indiana University Press.

He was injected with
estrogen hormones
rendering him impotent
his breasts growing soft
and large like a woman's.
With security access revoked
he was barred from his work
advancing the field of cryptography.

Two weeks before his 42nd birthday
he was found dead by his housecleaner
a half-eaten apple by his bedside
and speculation of suicide
by cyanide poisoning—
taken down by society.

Society called him sick and twisted.
Society, the great oppressor,
is sick and twisted
cold and unforgiving
restrained by lies and ties
to old church traditions.

ii. Desiring Machines

Despite our capacity for individual expression, desire is also highly influenced by the forces of *desiring machines*.[14] That is, throughout the course of universal history, successive *mega-machines* or social forms have organized, canalized, and repressed desire.[15] In this way, individual desire builds from unconscious drives, which are subject to the inescapable and pervasive intrusion of societal scripts, instructing us on who and how we should desire.

One of the most obvious and powerfully tenacious examples of this in recent western history is found in traditional male and female roles. The binary nature of gender scripts continues to get buy-in from many women who accept subordinate roles to men, despite their collective gains in work and economic realms. Men, who may not hold power positions in work and financial circles, often continue to *rule the roost* in the home.

"I could die for you.
But I couldn't, and wouldn't, live for you."[16]

---

[14] Desire theory of Gilles Deleuze and Pierre-Félix Guattari.

[15] Schuster, A. (2009). Drive and desire: Zizek and *Anti-Oedipus*. Jan van Eyck Circle for Lacanian Ideology website.

[16] Rand, Ayn. (1943). *The Fountainhead*.

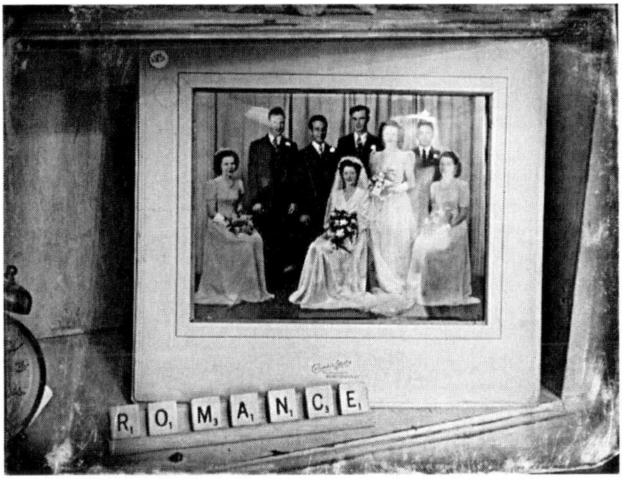
ROMANCE

Replications

When she was ten years old
her step-father moved into
their home at the end of the
Semlin Street cul-de-sac
disrupting the flow of life
for her, her sister, and her
hard-working mother who
struggled to make a living at
Woodwood's shoe department.

Having a step-father around
meant that her mother could spend
more time at home, an on-demand
housewife, cooking and cleaning
and taking care of the family;
theoretically
in truth
it meant more time
for drinking beer
and playing cards.

There were many restless nights
where she tucked herself under
the covers, lying quietly in bed
listening to the voices in the

living room as they got louder
with each beer cracked
with each cigarette lit
until her mother went to bed
worn out from the drunken chatter
and he came to her room
alcohol on his breath
evil on his hands.

Afterward, she would
soak in a hot bathtub
scrubbing down her brown
and drunkenly-touched skin
wishing it were white
the colour of rich girls
who she thought were never
touched by dirty old men
who were never invisible
to their stay-at-home mothers
who should have known
who chose to turn a blind eye
because of the pangs of
unbearable guilt rising to the surface
regretting the power slipping through
over-worked and under-paid fingers.

And now, all these years later
with a ten year-old daughter
of her own, beautiful and hopeful,
and three years out of a long
and turbulent relationship
that mirrors too many parallels
of her life on Semlin Street—
the only desire that remains
is the desire for peace
and solitude.

iii. Circular Movement

The circular philosophy of desire emphasizes the resolution of desire through a function of transcendence and movement toward Other.[17] Other is the "expression of a possible world"[18] or movement beyond existing states.

Paradoxically, resolution may be unattainable because of desire's *pseudo-immanence* quality (an experience within the subject's mind that has no effect outside of it). In other words, fulfillment is a mere *illusion of satiation* obscured by a temporary state of pleasure. Pleasure simply serves to calm desires.[18]

---

[17] Desire theory of Gilles Deleuze.

[18] Reynolds, J. (2008). Deleuze's other-structure: Beyond the master-slave dialectic, but at what cost? *Symposium: Canadian Journal of Continental Philosophy, 12*(1), 67-88.

Telepathic Illusion

Some time ago, just after you left
when my heart was still plump & red and
soft & smooth in its state of ignorant bliss
I would close my eyes and speak your name
I could feel you there, your energy around me,
certain of your return.

Wherever I was, when the desire to have you close
came upon me, I would draw upon your memory
to *feel* your presence in the here and now--
in the elevator on my way home
at my desk as I sipped my morning tea
on a soft chair as I stretched out to unravel the day
in my bed as I longed for your missing touch.

Now I know this was a mere illusion
a mechanism to calm desires
a panacea to cope with
the pangs of love withdrawal
a device to obscure the painful reality;
once departed, you were never there.
And I know this as I have moved on
to another place in time where
just thinking of my lover brings promise
that he will appear without illusion.

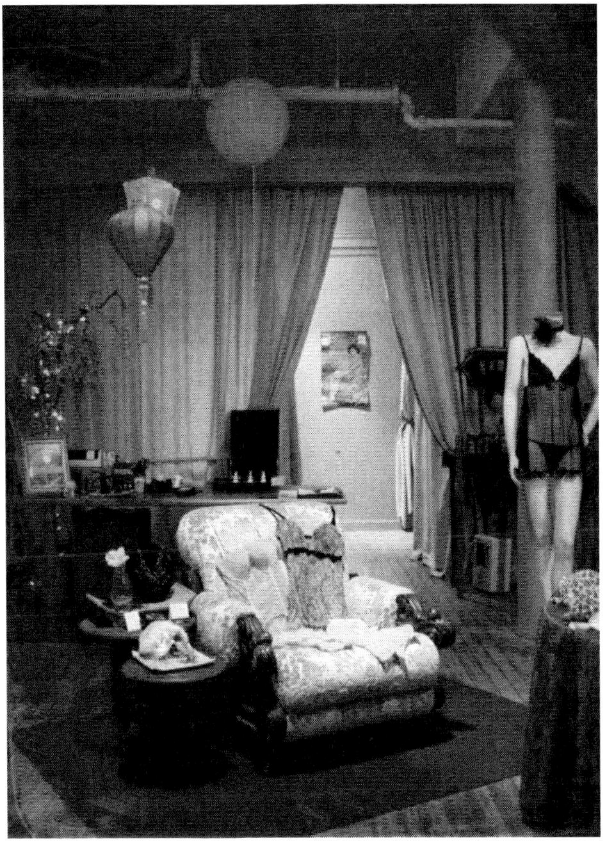

iv. Rational & Representative Desires

Although it can be said that our rational nature leads us toward end goals, the causes of our actions are never our desires or impulses.[19] Actions toward material goals are not freely taken; instead, they are intentional actions taken to satisfy a desire that is not always within our control.

Yet, sometimes our actions fail because our capacity to rationally shape our desires is limited. For example, we take action to find a life partner and live happily-ever-after (end goal), but because we often choose a partner based on internalized societal scripts of the kind of person we *think* we should be with, rather than a person who is actually a *better fit*, we end up with unsatisfied desires.

---

[19] Desire theory of Immanuel Kant, who is known for his philosophies of pure and practical reason.

Despite our rational nature, desire also has a representative function whereby sexual desire is nothing more than an animal inclination.[20] For example, sometimes a man's desire for a woman is not attributed to her true characteristics; instead, her sex is the object of his desire as sex represents the satiation of desire. In this sense, in its lower form, the products of desire are fantasies and superstitions,[21] and these sometimes serve as mere coping mechanisms for stress and distractions from the sometimes-difficult realities of life.

---

[20] Papadaki, E. (2007). Sexual objectification: From Kant to contemporary feminism. *Contemporary Political Theory, 6*, 330-348.

[21] Smith, D. (2007). Deleuze and the question of desire: Toward an immanent theory of ethics. *Parrhesia: A Journal of Critical Philosophy, 2*, 66-78.

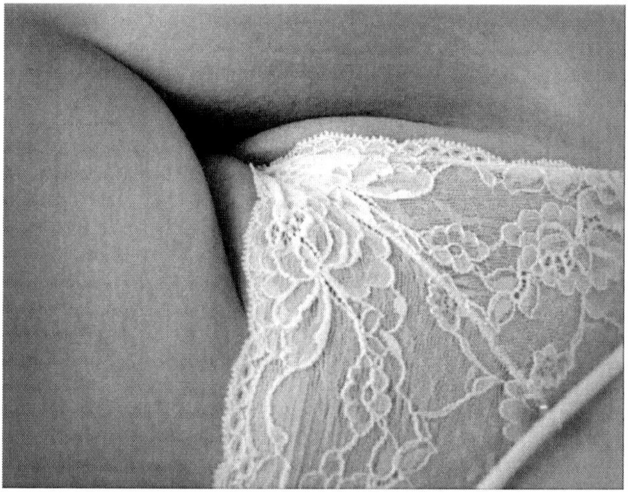

Secret Compartments

He has done all the right things:
he married his first love
his high school sweetheart
and now three children
and fifteen years in
sometimes when he looks
at his thirty-something bride
he feels cool distance and
pangs of resentment.

He has kept up
his end of the bargain
a corporate lawyer
bringing in decent money
to provide a beautiful home
and a comfortable life.
But her beauty has become
increasingly invisible to him.
What used to feel familiar
comfortable and complete
now feels confining
smothering him in such a way
that in quiet moments alone
he contemplates the voice
inside that screams "run".

Nicki works at the coffee shop
where he stops each morning.
Her bright eyes and open smile
greet him without judgment
until one day she mentions
it is her last as she is moving on.
Without hesitation
he asks for her number
tucking it away until
a few weeks pass
torn between discarding it
and using it.

After a long day
at the end of a rough week
he thought of her
(beautiful animal distraction)
and his fingers made the call.

She answered
with a smiling tone in her voice;
they chatted for while, until he
finessed the conversation toward
making plans to meet at her place.

He arrived late
but that was just fine
she was easy that way
chilling the wine and
sitting in the living room
smoking a cigarette
watching the half-moon
anticipating the night ahead.

He took off his jacket
and sat beside her...
her thick perfume
and large breasts in a
lacy white push-up bra
peeking though a sheer
tie-up blouse, calling to him.

He took her from behind
fucking her hot wet pussy
not risking that her lips
would want more than
he was willing to give.
The slapping sound
of skin on skin
making him thrust
harder and faster.

Later, that evening
as he left her place
walking to his car
he felt alive again
returned to a feeling
of unburdened satisfaction
yet beneath the calm of desire
he knew he would have to find
a way to keep his secret
under wraps, filing it away
in convoluted, guilt-ridden
desire-filled compartments.

v. Shapes & Connections: Self Returned From Other

Desire has a connective function; it shapes and connects interactions between self, others, and the world.[22] From this angle, desire is self-consciousness returned from others; it is "the unity of the "I" within itself",[23] while *other* or *otherness* refers to the separation between self and other.

Desire, then, does not drive us to fill a void within ourselves; instead, it confirms and enhances our sense of self. Desire is the movement of consciousness, not the absence of emptiness.

Yet, desire is also contradictory. Once satisfied, self-consciousness cannot remain in a state of self-certainty; instead it must again seek out new objects of desire to consume.[24] In this way, desire "affirms *itself as an impossible project.*"[25]

---

[22] Desire theory of G.W.F. Hegel.
[23] Houlgate, S. (1994). Chapter 1: G. W. F. Hegel: The phenomenology of spirit.
[24] Paradoxically, in dating scenarios, when individuals show romantic desire to others, those others tend *not* to desire in return (Eastwick, P., Finkel, E., et al (2007). Selective versus unselective romantic desire: Not all reciprocity is created equal. *Psychological Science, 18* (4), 317-319.
[25] Butler, J. (1990). *Gender trouble: Feminism and the subversion of identity.*

The Impossible Project

At the age of thirteen
the spirit of muse called upon you
in the form of Eddie Van Halen
and you began to play guitar.
The rhythm and the notes
filled a void of desire within you
a need to express, to connect
and to be valued by others.
And so you played on...
locked away for hours at a time
alone in your room, until the notes
became natural and knowing.

You travel the world
with your guitar, playing for the people
who want you, who want to *be* you
who make you feel loved, and hated,
that you are enough and never enough
cursed and hopelessly oppressed
alone in the shadows of self-doubt
yet driven to press onward into the
conquered and just-out-of-reach
Land of Arrival, set aside for
goddesses of sex & beauty
and deserving gods of guitar.

Your muse has returned from Other
to reaffirm the movement of your soul
blissfully soaring and often contradictory
yet never an absence or a void of
connection. It is merely the natural
and designed evolution of your soul;
your muse reaffirms these contradictions
so you seek out new objects
of desire to consume
wine and women
and new guitars
reinforcing the notion that
desire remains
the impossible project.

vi. To Know is to Desire

Experience is the source of all knowledge and conscious knowledge is always intentional.[26] Desire, which emerges as a form of consciousness, is also always intentional.[27]

The human mind functions with intention or direction toward an object (person), including emotions and desires, from consciousness, from a position of background (instincts and pleasure-seeking) or nearer to the pure ego (moral restraints and internalized cultural rules).[28] Imagine an angel sitting on one shoulder and a devil on the other and you have the ego's function: To mediate between the two forces.

We desire what we know, to reaffirm what we know.

---

[26] Desire theory of Edmund Husserl, an Austrian-born Jewish philosopher and founder of phenomenology, the philosophical study of the structures of subjective experience and consciousness.

[27] New World Encyclopedia. (2008). Edmund Husserl.

[28] Kockelmans, J. (1994). *Edmund Husserl's phenomenology.* Indiana: Purdue University Research Foundation.

The Arc of Possibilities

He had always been with
a certain kind of woman
young and pretty
long hair, tawny blonde
long legs in strapped stilettos
and curve-fitting jeans;
women who followed his band
religiously
but not schooled in music.

Until her.
Beautiful Persian skin, grey eyes and
long black hair, sassy and sophisticated
educated in London's finest schools;
she opened his eyes
to the theories of Nietzsche
and the poems of Chaucer.
No longer could desire be contained
to the immediacies of the skin
or blood pumping through veins
now that there was this language
between them
now that she had shown his tongue
to new and unknown territories.

A nomad, a career climber
she said their love was
a mere stepping stone
to expanded horizons.
So, as she kissed him,
his face cradled in her hands
(a freeze-frame moment
of remembering
what it felt like
before and after
she walked into
the city light distance)
he was left standing
knowing, in solitude
the arc of possibilities
leads back to him.

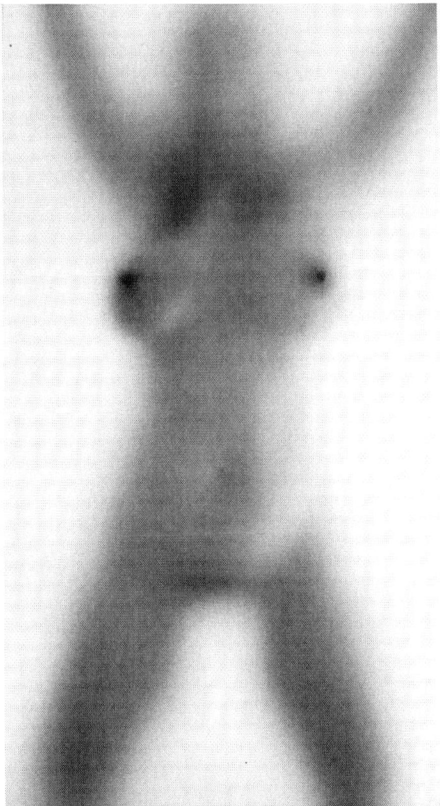

vii. Reflectivity & Desire

The human desire for others is not a universal truth.[29] Instead, aside from innate biological needs, we learn how and what to desire.[30] As children we attempt to satisfy these needs, but instead, we sometimes get caught up in our interactions with others.

As the sense of self develops from the identification with the images of these others, we learn to desire either directly, through another, or others. In this way, an object (person) may become more desirable when there is a perception that others desire it.

---

[29] Jacques Lacan's *Desire is the Desire of Other* theory from his *Mirror Stage* developmental concept of identity.
[30] Sharpe, M. (2005). *Jacques Lacan: Desire is the desire of the other.* Internet Encyclopedia of Philosophy.

Smoke & Mirrors

I remember you before the fame
you were just another shaggy-haired
hemp-wearing East Vancouver scenester
blending in with the neo-hippies
saving the environment, promoting
vegetarianism, drinking fair-trade coffee
hanging out on Commercial Drive.

For awhile, we shared a jam space
me, trying to channel Concrete Blonde
you writing acoustic songs about guns
bombs and geopolitics; sonic irony.
After you went electric
the record company vultures
swarmed down with greedy claws
they amped up your sound
glossed up your pictures
and the groupie frenzy followed.

Interviewed by a local journalist
you were asked about your new-found
sex appeal and desirability, laughing
with skepticism, you said, "That's insane,
I just keep writing songs 'cause one day
the truth will be revealed."

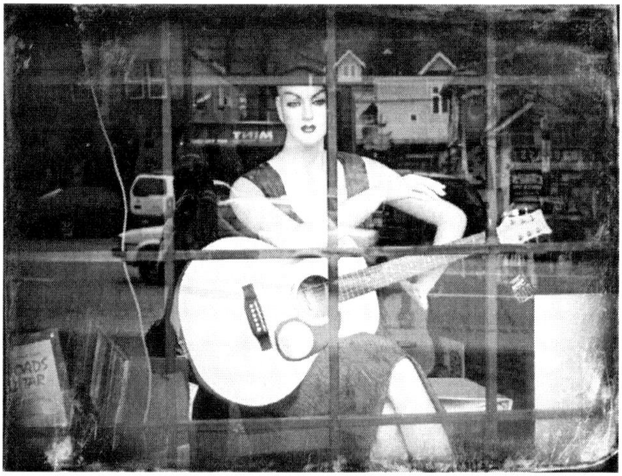

viii. Altering Desire

Only those with indifference in their heart forego the need to connect with others. Yet, when our biological needs become inseparable or subordinated to the demand for recognition and love from others the *decentring* of desire occurs. Consequently, we alter our decisions regarding wants and desires in order to affect and be affected by the decisions of others.[31]

"If I didn't define myself for myself,
I would be crunched into
other people's fantasies for me
and eaten alive."[32]

---

[31] Sharpe, M. (2005). *Jacques Lacan: Desire is the desire of the other.* Internet Encyclopedia of Philosophy.
[32] Audre Lorde.

Always Moving On

In the moment that she followed him
downstairs, the dark, gloomy heaviness
of her childhood reappeared:
She was thirteen years old
living with an aunt after the
tension between her parents
became too much to bear.

She returned home one day
to find empty rooms, the memories
of home hollowed out and empty like
her voice as she called to her
mother and father, in her heart
a sinking, fretful feeling, knowing
they were gone, on the run again
Kingston-bound, without a note
without a word or a phone call.

He had the eyes of her father
black and knowing, but hardened
by a life that didn't go as planned
always bailing just before things
could turn around, could make a turn
for the better.

The next morning, beside him
the distance between their
bodies now cool and divided
past memories fall forward
to the dream where she's standing
beside someone strong & steady who
would lift her heart from the torn
grey pattern of her past, but
now in the stark light of day
the temporary fix of last night
crashed down hard with a
concrete sense of reality.

She felt returned to her childhood room abandoned,
with its broken shade and
creaky wooden floor, neglected, but
pointless to fix, as soon everything
would surge in crescendo and return to
its default state of perpetual motion...
Moving on.

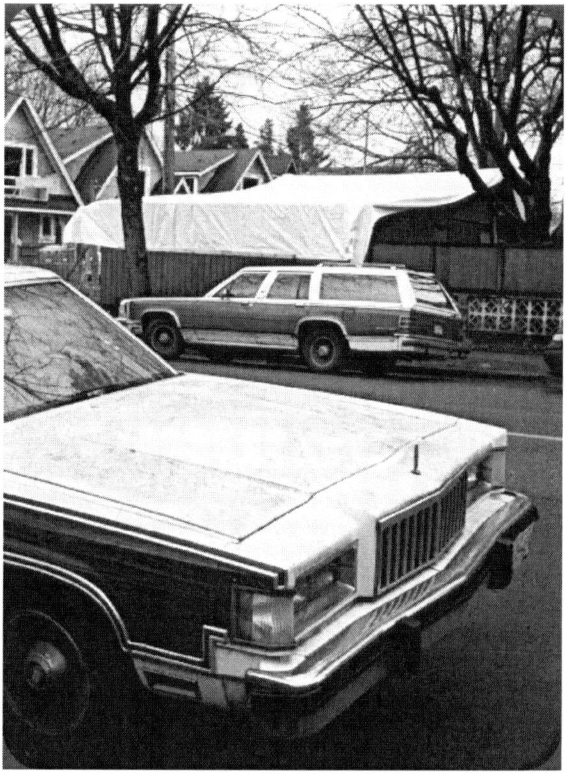

ix. Dreams & Desires

The theories of Sigmund Freud, particularly his theory of dreams, continue to live on, transcending the field of psychology, and influencing diverse genres of esoteric thinking, including art, film, literature, and music.[33] Freud's theory of desire draws from his concepts of dreams and the unconscious, where dreams are fulfillments of wishes (desire) and desire is a *cathexis* (a concentration of emotional energy on an object).[34]

Freud also believed that desire is only satisfied once; subsequent manifestations of desire are impulses that seek to re-establish the image of a lost object, sometimes to the point of (psychotic) hallucination. Dreams, then, serve the purpose of expressing the attainment of desires.[35]

---

[33] For example, Jim Morrison, singer for *The Doors* alluded to Freud's concept of the Oedipus Complex in the song *The End* (1968).
[34] Thornton, S. (2010). Sigmund Freud. Internet Encyclopedia of Philosophy.
[35] Delaroche, P. (n.d.). Subject's desire. Gale Dictionary of Psychoanalysis.

Cathexix

It was more than a dozen years ago
and yet much like yesterday when
I was taken down, trapped by the darkness
in my own head, sinking into a downward spiral
so low I buckled helplessly at the knees.
   I came to you in desperation and
      in a last ditch attempt at grace
         composed my fragile body on your
            grey velvet psychiatrist couch
               certain that all the weathered books
               on your shelf would hold answers.

      It was my premature assumption that
      you could unlock the hidden secrets
of my lithium-pacified existence
as you were in control, but your soul
  was more deeply damaged than my own.
Slowly, awkwardly, without grace
and without my initial detection
you realize that I hold all the answers to
your grave state of emptiness and now
there is no boundary to mark the line
between my needs and yours, so
willingly and blindly, I cross over.

And then it came to this:
I want to purge myself of you
but I still carry part of you in
hauntingly random appearances
in frantic and unfinished moments
and peaceful times of reflection.

My wise friends said that one day
I would merely be amused by
my foolish investment in you.
This day came after much
time had swelled with distance
and yet lurking somewhere
in the corners of my mind
you occasionally revisit
a deeply carved presence
absorbed in me, unfinished
vaguely visible, but raised
like faded keloid tissue.

Now your closed silence
serves as parting words
even though something within me
knows you will return one day
with a booming and undeniable roar
haunting me from within my dreams
the one where I am stalked by a lion
saved by a wise old woman
who resembles me
then softly cradled
like a newborn baby.

Dreams give us more than we ask—
glimpses into a deeper meaning,
embedded within the dream, symbolically,
in the form of archetypal images
looming within the collective unconscious.[36]

---

[36] Jung, Carl J. (1971). Modern man in search of a soul. (W.S. Dell and Cary F. Baynes, Trans.). Harcourt, Brace & World: New York. (Original work published 1933).

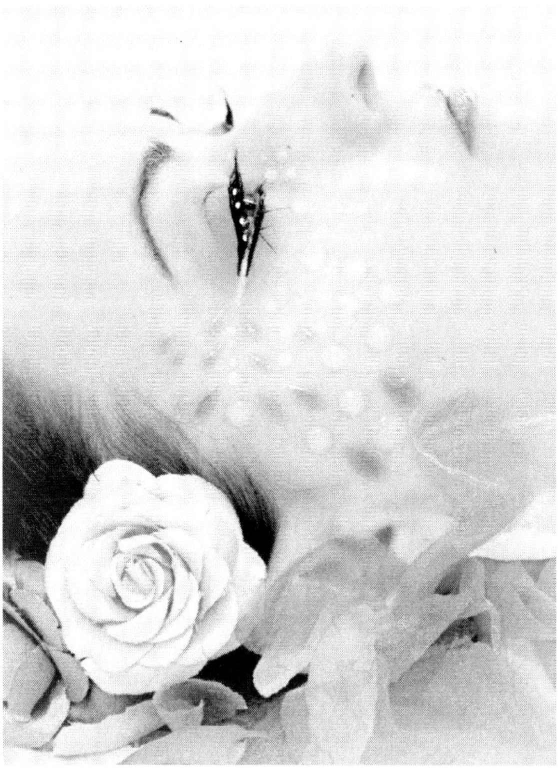

Virtuosity and Madness:
A Story of Unrequited Love
(in honour of Josef Hassid, 1923-1950)

(1923)
Hassid, born the third of four children
to a poor Jewish family living in Warsaw,
gravitated to the violin; self-taught until
the age of ten when his immense talent
was gifted to the rest of the world.

In brilliant musical virtuosity
the strings of the violin resonate
and embody the purity of the soul.

(1938)
Five years had passed
since the death of his mother
and the stages of London embraced
his luminous interpretations;
the turning point, an unrequited love
culminations of tensions and stage fright.

Exposed to the world
the strings of his violin resonate
with the vibrations of a soul
touched by outer forces.

(1941)
Eight timeless recordings
capture the once-solidified promise
of the trajectory of genius
brought to a standstill
by the manifestation of psychosis
in pre-chlorpromazine times.

(1950)
Seven years caged in London asylums
wandering aimlessly, restrained, violent resistance
detached, laughing inanely, musically severed
sixty insulin comas, sullen and solitary,
a schizophrenic soul murder.[37]

A post-lobotomized death;
in life his music continues to resonate
and within this genius, there is no final silence.

---

[37] Feinstein, A. (1997). Psychosurgery and the child prodigy: The mental illness of violin virtuoso Josef Hassid. *History of Psychiatry, 8.* pp.55-60

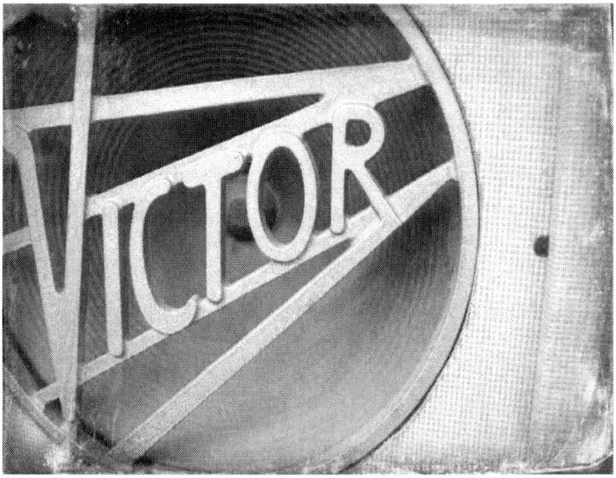
VICTOR

x. Freudian Shortcomings

Freud believed that gender develops alongside sexual identity, desire, and personality, in conjunction with biological sex and mature heterosexuality. Gender, then, fuses into one multi-faceted expression of core identity (male or female), including gender roles and sexual orientation.[38]

Alternatively, because Freud's theory is framed from a position of male superiority and heterosexual desire, it has been vigorously disputed by, among others, feminists and contemporary social theorists.

"...the man of my dreams is a girl." [39]

---

[38] Shields, S., & Eyssell, M. (2002). History of the study of gender psychology. In N. Levvy & B. Makinister (Eds.). *Encyclopedia of women and gender: Sex similarities and differences and the impact of society on gender* (pp.597-600). San Diego, CA: Academic Press.

[39] Peters, Julie Anne. (2005). *Keeping you a secret.*

One challenge to Freud's theory views gender identity and desire as temporal constructs. That is, each reflects learned but variable behavior over time, expressed in thought, language, and the body.[40]

Similarly, a gender continuum of sexuality and desire beyond biological factors accounts for how gender and desire coincide in fluid contexts. This means the expression of each develops from cultural influences and individual experiences. In this sense, gender and desire are potentially impermanent.[40]

---

[40] Butler, J. (1990). *Gender trouble: Feminism and the subversion of identity.*

88

In Honour of Woman

His desire for her touch grew from
a primitive and unquestioned need
to possess someone too compliant
and powerless to resist, and given her
brown skin and history of stolen language
he knew, she had not yet found a voice to defy.

For him, moments of tenderness
came only when his guard was
dulled down after a few drinks
or his libido primed up after
a few more drinks.
At first she accepted this
as her plight, a legacy of
restraint, held back
just like her mother
married to a white man
now waiting for the healing
of the Tsimshian people
seven generations to come.

Later, she felt shame
for the history of oppression
that chained her Native people
to repeated generations

of colonial obsession.
Over time and the waning of hope
she felt anger consume her
followed by waves of repulsion
for ever touching the skin of
another *civilized* white oppressor.

Her kind and forgiving nature only
made her hold on to him tighter
but loving his hard shell
to soften him only made her
grow tired and distant.

Now in the arms of a woman
with tender brown eyes of strength
and thick lashes that tilt downwards
in moments of compassion and reflection
and strong hands that lead to warm luscious places
but never say follow, never say wait
with soft open lips over her desiring breasts
in a way that makes her touch herself with
quiet pleasure after she is gone, anticipating her
return home again when they will share
after-dinner coffee at the kitchen table
talking about the events of the day
until night calls them back into
each other's arms.

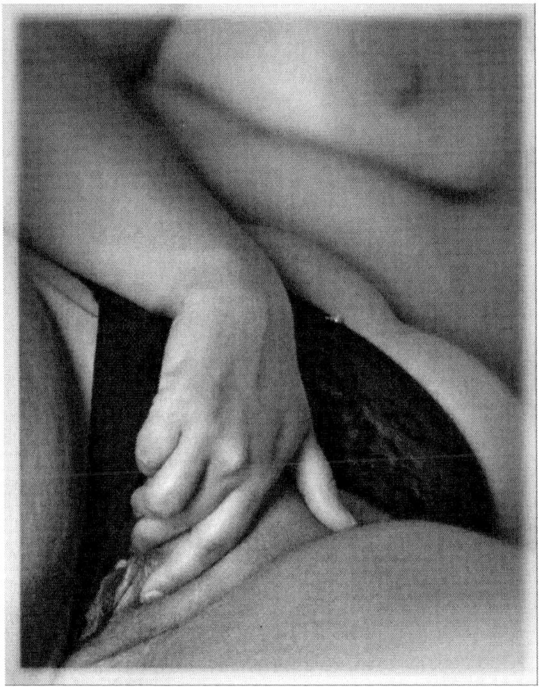

Desire and Artistic Expression

What separates the human mind from other life forms is the ability to create, to use imagination, and visualize movement beyond existing states. Undeniably, "our visions begin with our desires."[41]

Acts of creativity also interlink with various forms of desire. At one end of the spectrum, desire expressed in art is known as sublimation,[42] or the channeling of unwanted impulses into creative outlets. Rather than repressing desire into the unconscious, channeling desire through substitute activities brings greater satisfaction. Yet, the notion that art only expresses unconscious motives reduces it to a neurosis.[43] More commonly, the desire to create coincides with acquired desires, such as lover's desire, the desire to connect with others, and the expression of our experiences with those who leave permanent and powerful imprints on our hearts. Undoubtedly, the beauty of love songs, paintings, and poetry, both historical and contemporary, can be traced to their inspiration from desire, unrequited love, or loss of love, as their muse.

---

[41] Audre Lorde.
[42] Gay, Volney P. (1992). Freud on sublimation: Reconsiderations. New York State University of New York Press.
[43] Gay, Volney P. (1992). p.12

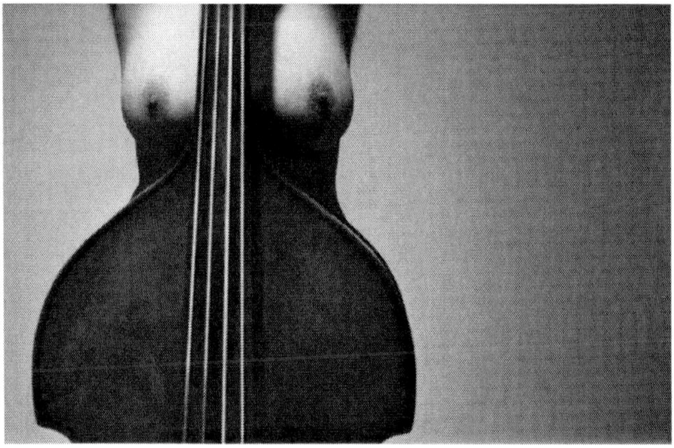

Behind These Walls – Dream Completion

Behind these walls
there looms a history
an industrious time
grounded in layers
of concrete pillars
and wood-planked floor.

With the warmth
of your body-snuggled quilt
you rise to a brutally cold
November dawn, awakened by
a train rumbling past, its wheels
pounding icy tracks.

The aroma of coffee
fills the chilly morning air
as you gaze through
a frost-framed window
to a tangle of distant silhouettes
the landscape of the city.

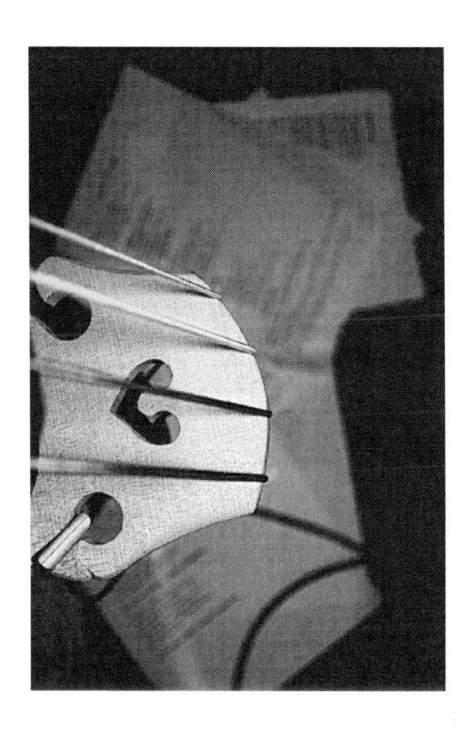

Behind these walls
is where you have always known
your destiny would lie
painting life as it channels from
new streams of consciousness
awaiting canvas; dream completion
desire completion.

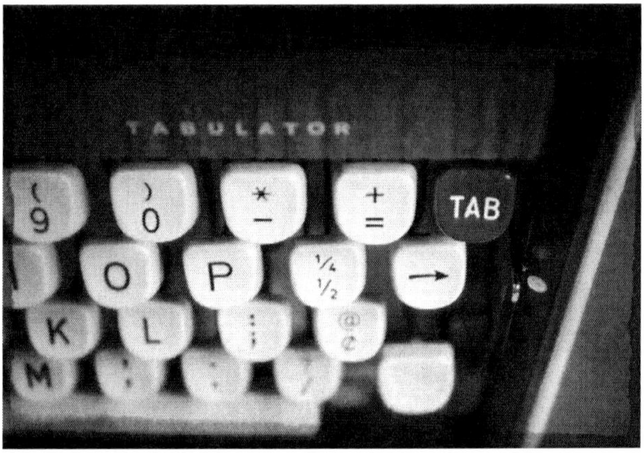
TABULATOR
TAB
9
0
O
P
K
L
M

Desire and the Changing Seasons

Across the changing seasons, there is something distinct about the expression of desire. Winter brings a kind of quiescence to desire. By the time December rolls around, desire drapes quietly between lovers as they sit by the fire enjoying hot chocolate, each reading a book, the weather so dark and grim they have no inclination to venture out into the cold night. On Sunday mornings they sleep late, comfortable in each other's arms, listening to the rain pummel the roof, with no guilt about their slow-rising morning.

In the springtime, thankful for longer days, lovers enjoy coffee or dinner on outdoor patios, or after dinner walks by the ocean. With the bloom of spring flowers, desire, too, has a renewed energy. Taking in this new energy, we are more inclined to reinvigorate care and attention to our mind, spirit and body, and, consequently, attract like-minded lovers.

Summertime brings weekends at the beach, relaxing under a wide umbrella, sipping cold drinks, and planning vacations. Soon after the June solstice arrives, desire, too, seems to peak. Here we feel most alive and want to share this burgeoning energy with our lover.

The cooler days of autumn bring long drives to the country, taking the time to revel in the beauty of the season's changing colours. Knowing that winter is about to descend, fall is a time for reflection, sharing a glass of wine between lovers, watching the sun set a little sooner each night, enjoying the last run of fair weather before the long stretch of cold winter days arrive, and the cycle of desire begins again.

At Last, Cherry Blossoms

Around the time
of the killing frost
when the days grew shorter
and the cold autumn skies
cast a bruised-grey backdrop
against a field of
abandoned pumpkins
and withering corn stalks
once tall like scarecrows
he left this world by his own taking.

Afterward,
the days seemed endless
as she paced the floors
of their empty house
(no longer a home)
pleading to God
praying for an end
to the crippling
curse of pain.

Night after night
the wine bottles and
take-out containers
piled up like collapsed hope
as she shut out the world
curled up in a fetal position
on their bed, now ghostlike
and empty without him.

After New Year's day
friends called to check in
to comfort themselves with
news that she was moving on.
She found the words
to appease their need
until resentment set in
her tired and heavy bones.
With her weary heart broken
and overburdened with pain
she crumbled to the floor
at the foot of the bed.
There was no way to move on
 except through sleep (when it came)
when she was closed off
from the reality of facing
the world alone.

At last, the cherry blossoms came.
She drove by the ocean
to their favourite spot
a triangle of trees
pink and new
remembering him
and old dreams
of the future.

She walked by
a beach-front café
and gazed into the window
where they used to sit;
now there was a new kind of pain
one mixed with distance
acceptance and resolution.

Standing on the edge
of the pebbled pathway
to the beach, she watched
the pink cherry blossoms
shake loose from their branches
cast to the wind
taking with them
all notions of loss
accepting all blessings
of the new season.

Closing Thoughts

What kind of journey is desire that its direction is often deceptive?[44]

How can we resolve desire's greatest contradiction? ... it pulls us one way while societal forces often lead us in another.

Does desire have other stops before it reaches its destination?

I believe so, many stops. Some stops will be bitterly painful, some seemingly soul-defeating and some soul-elevating. Still, other stops, despite their temporary nature, will be deeply defining.

Yet, although desire is often "immediate, arbitrary, purposeless, and animal,"[44] on another level it is intricately connected with the quest for self-knowledge and the pursuit of identity in what seems to be distantly familiar. Only when something external to our consciousness is discovered within, when the "transformation of difference into identity"[44] completes will desire truly be satisfied. In other words, when the strange becomes familiar, when the awaited

---

[44] Butler, J. (1987). *Subjects of desire. Hegelian reflections in twentieth-century France.* New York: Columbia University Press.

arrives, when the lost re-emerges, and when resolution takes hold.

Despite desire's capacity to be a powerful force in our lives, across our lives, we do have choice. That is, although the source of our passionate desires is often emotion, we can take comfort in knowing our instrumental desires materialize from our intellect, our consciousness.[45] Desires form through an imperfect collaboration between these two sources.

When desire takes you to dark places
reach for the light.

In my introduction I expressed my intent to explore the fluid layers of desire to reveal its shape-shifting quality, which changes over time, history, and with love gained or lost. Seeking to explore dimensions that you may recognize in your own desire journey, I also travelled to many raw and often unspoken layers of desire. Whether you find links between desire and addiction, trauma, power, or some other manifestation, I hope you find temporary resolution in desire's deceptive and contradictory nature, as well as pleasure in its ability to amuse and inspire with its seemingly

---

[45] Irvine, W. (2006). *On desire: Why we want what we want.* New York: Oxford University Press.

random ability to interrupt the flow of life with the element of surprise. Finally, I hope that within these pages you find traces of your own desire history, which awakens new understanding of your own subtext. Herein lies the true power of desire.

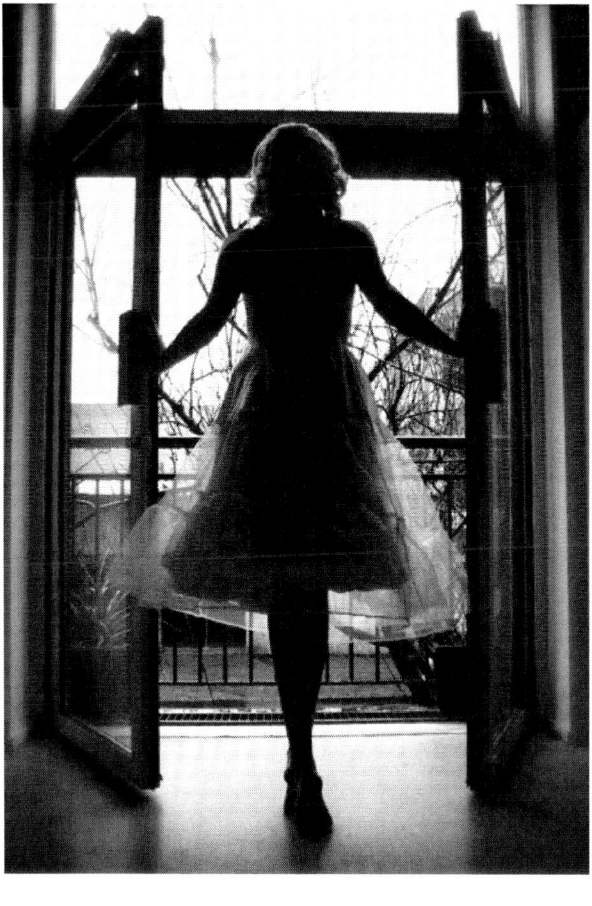

I was born in New Westminster, British Columbia to a German father and a French-Cree-Métis mother who instilled in me the drive to make all my creative visions reality. I now call Vancouver home.

Despite well-intentioned suppression by elementary school teachers, I have loved poetry since the third grade. Although there have been many years in between songwriting and playing guitar in alternative rock bands, pursuing an undergraduate degree in psychology and a graduate degree in cultural studies, in this collection, I return to poetry, my first love. At last, I revisit an old and cherished friend.

Graciously,

Kim Bayer
Vancouver, BC
Canada

Photo by Lisa Bayer
www.lisabayer.com